West African CUISINE

Enslow PUBLISHING

COOKING WITH CULTURE

BY JUDY THORPE

Please visit our website, www.enslow.com. For a free color catalog of all our high-quality books, call toll free 1-800-398-2504 or fax 1-877-980-4454.

Library of Congress Cataloging-in-Publication Data
Names: Thorpe, Judy, author.
Title: West African cuisine / Judy Thorpe.
Description: Buffalo, New York : Enslow Publishing, [2025] | Series: Cooking with culture | Includes index.
Identifiers: LCCN 2024003392 | ISBN 9781978540514 (library binding) | ISBN 9781978540507 (paperback) | ISBN 9781978540521 (ebook)
Subjects: LCSH: Cooking, African–Juvenile literature. | Food–Africa, West–History–Juvenile literature. | LCGFT: Cookbooks.
Classification: LCC TX725.A4 T45 2025 | DDC 641.5966–dc23/eng/20240212
LC record available at https://lccn.loc.gov/2024003392

Published in 2025 by
Enslow Publishing
2544 Clinton Street
Buffalo, NY 14224

Portions of this work were originally authored by Ethan Y. Garten and published as *Foods of West Africa*. All new material in this edition authored by Judy Thorpe.

Designer: Leslie Taylor
Editor: Caitie McAneney

Photo credits: Cover (photo) Linda Hughes Photography/Shutterstock.com; Series Art (background icon pattern) porcelaniq/Shutterstock.com; Series Art (series logo) lukeruk/Shutterstock.com; p. 5 Tolu Owoeye/Shutterstock.com; p. 7 Aimee Lee Studios/Shutterstock.com; p. 9 William Borney/Shutterstock.com; p. 11 Fanfo/Shutterstock.com; p. 13 Lekan Agboola/Shutterstock.com; p. 15 shynebellz/Shutterstock.com; p. 17 Stockphoto5/Shutterstock.com; p. 19 Ezume Images/Shutterstock.com; p. 21 Thao Lan/Shutterstock.com.

Printed in the United States of America

CPSIA compliance information: Batch #CSENS25: For further information contact Enslow Publishing at 1-800-398-2504.

Contents

Words in the glossary appear in **bold** type the first time they are used in the text.

Discover West Africa

West Africa is a land of grasslands, rain forests, coastline, and dry earth. This **region** has the Atlantic Ocean to the west and the Sahara Desert to the north. There are many mainland countries here, as well as island countries such as Cape Verde.

FOOD FOR THOUGHT

THE COUNTRIES OF WEST AFRICA INCLUDE BENIN, BURKINA FASO, CAMEROON, CAPE VERDE, CHAD, GAMBIA, GHANA, GUINEA, GUINEA-BISSAU, IVORY COAST, LIBERIA, MALI, MAURITANIA, NIGER, NIGERIA, SENEGAL, SIERRA LEONE, AND TOGO.

Food is an important part of community and **celebration** in West Africa.

Many different groups of people have lived in West Africa throughout history. There are many **cultures**, and they all add to the rich flavor of West African **cuisine**. Over time, this cuisine has spread around the world.

Food on the Move

West African cuisine was shaped by the trade of enslaved people. Arabs arrived in Africa over 2,000 years ago. They traded spices, **herbs**, and salt to Africans for gold, ivory, and enslaved people.

FOOD FOR THOUGHT

THE AMERICAN SOUTH'S CUISINE INCLUDES MANY WEST AFRICAN FOODS SUCH AS SESAME SEEDS, **OKRA**, AND BLACK-EYED PEAS.

Gumbo is a popular food in Louisiana. Its name comes from the word for "okra" in several West African languages.

Later, Europeans sailed to West Africa. In return for enslaved people, they offered plants from the Americas such as peanuts, plantains, chili peppers, and corn. The European traders took African crops to the Americas. Enslaved West Africans tried to keep their **customs** alive in the Americas.

An Important Meal

Many people in West Africa eat a large evening meal. It's a time for families, neighbors, and friends to sit down and share news. The evening meal is cooked in one pot.

This one-pot meal is often mostly made up of vegetables such as corn, cassava, or yams.

FOOD FOR THOUGHT

CASSAVA IS A PLANT WITH LARGE ROOTS THAT CAN BE EATEN.

Kola nuts are an important part of West African cuisine. People eat them each day for health and energy.

Rice and other grains, such as millet, may be added. People either scoop up the food with their fingers or use pieces of bread. They use their right hand to eat.

Using Animals For Food

Many dishes in West Africa are cooked without meat. That's because many people can't afford it. However, meals for special celebrations may include meat such as chicken, goat, lamb, or beef. West Africans who live in cities tend to eat more meat.

Africans who raise livestock most often use them for milk and cheese, not for meat.

Fish stew is a common meal in Nigeria.

West African farmers use cows' milk to make a sour food that's much like yogurt. It's called *nunu*.

FOOD FOR THOUGHT

STEWS, OR MIXES OF VEGETABLES AND MEAT, ARE POPULAR DISHES IN WEST AFRICA. OXTAIL STEW IS MADE FROM THE MEAT FOUND ON THE TAIL OF A COW.

Bring the Flavor

Root vegetables are important crops in West Africa. However, these vegetables don't have much **flavor** on their own. Spices bring the flavor!

The spice called grains of paradise comes from the seeds of the melegueta pepper.

FOOD FOR THOUGHT

ANOTHER IMPORTANT **INGREDIENT** OF WEST AFRICAN CUISINE IS PALM OIL. IT'S USED THE WAY BUTTER AND OIL ARE USED IN OTHER CUISINES.

A flavorful West African food is the plantain, which looks like a banana. Plantains can be fried, boiled, baked, or grilled.

It tastes a bit like black pepper and ginger combined. Other spices include paprika, crushed red pepper, ginger, and cinnamon. Spices can be used to season meat. They can be added to stews and rice dishes.

Spice Is Nice!

Some West African dishes are very spicy! This heat is often from chili peppers. *Piri-piri* means "pepper-pepper" in the African language of Swahili. It's also what many Africans call the bird's-eye chili. Another popular chili pepper in West Africa is the scotch bonnet.

FOOD FOR THOUGHT

STAYING COOL IS IMPORTANT IN THE EXTREME HEAT OF WEST AFRICA. WEST AFRICA IS HOME TO SOME OF THE HOTTEST COUNTRIES ON EARTH.

These chili peppers are for sale at a market in Lagos, Nigeria.

Besides adding flavor to a dish, chili peppers offer another interesting benefit. Eating hot peppers makes people sweat. Sweating helps cool a body down on a hot day.

Pass the Fufu!

Swallow foods are important in West African cuisine. A swallow food often goes along with a meal. It is soft and stretchy, and it is not supposed to be chewed.

Fufu (or foo foo) is a swallow made of yams, plantains, cassavas, and other vegetables. These are cooked and crushed into a paste.

FOOD FOR THOUGHT

IT TAKES A LOT OF TIME TO MAKE FUFU. THE MIX MUST BE POUNDED UNTIL IT CAN BE SWALLOWED WITHOUT BEING CHEWED.

Swallow foods include amala, eba, fufu, and poundo.

To eat fufu the West African way, a bit of the paste is rolled into a ball. It is served alongside a stew or soup. Dip the fufu and then enjoy!

Peanut Dishes

When many people think of West African stew, they think of peanut stew. Peanuts, tomatoes, onions, and chili peppers are cooked together in a pot. Sometimes meat is added.

Today, peanuts are found in many West African dishes. They are a great addition to sauces, soups, and stews. They're **roasted** and eaten as snacks.

FOOD FOR THOUGHT

PORTUGUESE TRADERS PROBABLY BROUGHT PEANUTS TO WEST AFRICA FROM SOUTH AMERICA IN THE 1560S. BY THE 1600S, PEANUTS WERE GROWING VERY SUCCESSFULLY.

They're pounded into peanut butter too. Peanut butter can be used to make a dish thicker.

Favorite Foods

Jollof is one of the most popular dishes in West Africa. It is made from another important crop—rice. Rice is mixed with meat or fish, tomatoes, onions, and spices in one pot.

A favorite food in West Africa is puff puff. This is a fried dough treat. Another food eaten as dessert is *thiakry*, which is a sweet, creamy dish topped with nuts and dried fruits. You can discover many new flavors and spices with West African cuisine!

Puff Puff

Ingredients

3 cups flour
1/4 cup sugar
2 cups warm water
2 1/2 teaspoons instant dry yeast
1/2 teaspoon salt
1/2 teaspoon nutmeg
Oil for frying

Equipment

mixing bowl
wooden spoon
measuring cups and spoons
clean kitchen towel
plastic wrap
large pot

Steps

1. Pour water into a large mixing bowl. Next, add sugar and yeast. Use a wooden spatula to mix well until it dissolves. Leave it for five minutes.
2. Add flour, salt, and nutmeg to the bowl. Mix until it become stretchy and soft.
3. Cover the bowl with plastic wrap and a dish towel for one hour.
4. With an adult's help, cover the bottom of a large pot in oil. Heat the oil over medium heat.
5. Drop lumps of batter the size of golf balls into the pot. Cook them until golden brown. Turn the balls to make sure they are deep fried on both sides.
6. Once golden brown, take the puff puff from the oil and transfer it to a plate with a paper towel on it to cool.

Glossary

celebration: A time to show happiness for an event through activities such as eating or playing music.

cuisine: A style of cooking.

culture: A group of people who share beliefs and ways of life.

custom: A way of doing things that is usual among the people in a certain group or place.

flavor: A feature of a food or drink that gives it a special taste.

herb: A low-growing plant used to add flavor to food.

ingredient: A part of a mixture.

okra: A plant that grows in warm places and has green pods that can be eaten.

region: A large area of land that has features that make it different from nearby areas of land.

roast: To heat a food until it is dry or brown.

For More Information

Books

Chambers, Catherine. *Slavery*. London, UK: Franklin Watts, 2021.

Klepeis, Alicia. *Nigeria*. Buffalo, NY: Cavendish Square Publishing, 2023.

Websites

Nigeria
kids.nationalgeographic.com/geography/countries/article/nigeria
Explore Nigeria with National Geographic Kids.

Sahara Desert
www.ducksters.com/history/africa/sahara_desert.php
Discover amazing facts about the largest hot desert on Earth.

Publisher's note to educators and parents: Our editors have carefully reviewed these websites to ensure that they are suitable for students. Many websites change frequently, however, and we cannot guarantee that a site's future contents will continue to meet our high standards of quality and educational value. Be advised that students should be closely supervised whenever they access the internet.

Index